How to Get Recognized, Re-Booked, and Referred

A Demystified Guide to Marketing Your Massage Practice

Nancy James

First Edition

Published by

The Aloha Touch System

Maui, Hawaii

I dedicate this book to my father, Daniel Nelson, who left our world too soon. I am looking forward to our reunion in heaven.

Acknowledgements

First and foremost I give thanks to the Lord because believing and trusting in him makes all things possible. I am grateful for a loving god who has infused in all of us some of his creative power so we may all live in abundance.

To my daughter Suhaila James who reminds me to be the best I can everyday and to live in the moment. I am so blessed to be your mother.

To my mother Mary Ziegler, who is the hardest worker I know. You have instilled in me a strong tenacity and desire for greatness.

To John Eggan, Thank you for believing in the need for this work, and giving me the tools to make it a reality.

To Theresa Doulliard, Thank you for your support and encouragement at every step of the way. You have a gift of bringing out the best in people.

To Tiffany Powell, Thank you for entrusting me with your business and giving me the freedom to grow.

To the contributing authors; Rosa Say, Tommy Wyatt and Curtis Lewsey & Dr. Ivan Misner I appreciate your permission to include your work. Thank you for being inspirational.

Thank you to all my clients throughout the years who have supported my practice, without you, none of this would be possible.

Thank you to all the "eyes" who have reviewed this manuscript and have given me valuable feedback. I am grateful for all of you!

How to Get Recognized, Re-booked, and Referred:
A Demystified Guide to Marketing Your Massage Practice

Introduction: The Meaning of Aloha & 19 Values of Aloha	
Chapter 1: Who this Book is For	13
Chapter 2: Making Your Marketing Personal	25
Chapter Three: Identifying, Finding, and Relating to Your Ideal Clients	43
Chapter Four: Differentiating Yourself from Your Competition	59
Chapter Five: Websites and Blogs	77
Chapter Six: Social Media	92
Chapter Seven: Freebies; How to Keep from Giving Too Much Away	105
Chapter Eight: Creative Ways to Fill Your Appointment Book	122
Chapter Nine: Conclusion	143
Resources	

The Meaning of Aloha

"And wherever [the native Hawaiian] went he said 'Aloha' in meeting or in parting. 'Aloha' was a recognition of life in another. If there was life there was mana, goodness and wisdom, and if there was goodness and wisdom there was a god-quality.

One had to recognize the 'god of life' in another before saying 'Aloha,'

but this was easy. Life was everywhere-- in the trees, the flowers,

the ocean, the fish, the birds, the pili grass, the rainbow, the rock--in all the world was life--was god--was Aloha. Aloha in its gaiety, joy, happiness, abundance.

Because of Aloha, one gave without thought of return; because of Aloha, one had mana. Aloha had its own mana. It never left the giver but flowed freely and continuously between giver and receiver. 'Aloha' could not be thoughtlessly or indiscriminately spoken, for it carried its own power. No Hawaiian could greet another with 'Aloha' unless he felt it in his own heart. If he felt anger or hate in his heart he had to cleanse himself before he said 'Aloha'."

Helena G. Allen, The Betrayal of Liliuokalani, Last Queen of Hawaii, 1838-1917. (Mutual Publishing: Honolulu)

The 19 Values of Aloha

Reprinted with permission from the book *Managing with Aloha* by Rosa Say

ALOHA—
Aloha is a value, one of unconditional love.
Aloha is the outpouring and receiving of the spirit.
HOʻOHANA—
The value of work: To work with intent and with purpose.
ʻIMI OLA—
To "seek best life." Our purpose in life is to seek its highest form.
The value of mission and vision.
HOʻOMAU—
The value of perseverance. To persist, to continue, to perpetuate. Never give up.
KŪLIA I KA NUʻU—
The value of achievement. "Strive to reach the summit."

Pursue personal excellence in all you do.
HOʻOKIPA—
The value of hospitality, a hospitality of complete giving.
Welcome guests and strangers with your spirit of Aloha.
ʻOHANA—
Those who are family, and those you choose to call your family.
As a value, ʻOhana is a human circle of complete Aloha.
LŌKAHI—
The value of teamwork: Collaboration and cooperation. Harmony and unity.
People who work together can achieve more.
KĀKOU—
The value of communication, for "All of us." We are in this together.
Learn to speak the language of we.
KULEANA—
One's personal sense of responsibility.
"I accept my responsibilities, and I will be

held accountable."

'IKE LOA—
The value of learning. To know well. To seek knowledge and wisdom.

HA'AHA'A—
The value of humility. Be humble, be modest, and open your thoughts.

HO'OHANOHANO—
To honor the dignity of others. Conduct yourself with distinction, and cultivate respectfulness.

ALAKA'I—
The value of leadership. Lead with initiative, and with your good example. You shall be the guide for others when you have gained their trust and respect.

MĀLAMA—
The value of stewardship. To take care of. To serve and to honor, to protect and care for.

MAHALO—
"Thank you", as a way of living. Live in thankfulness for the richness that

makes life so precious.

NĀNĀ I KE KUMU—
Look to your Sense of Place and sources of spirit, and you find your truth.

PONO—
The value of integrity, of rightness and balance.
The feeling of contentment when all is good and all is right.

KA LĀ HIKI OLA—
"The dawning of a new day." Optimism. The value of hope and promise.

Chapter 1: Who this book is for

Is this you?

Is your massage practice struggling to find clients?

Are you lacking clients that consistently rebook appointments with you?

Not earning much money & struggling to get by?

I want you to know, that **it's not your fault & I've been there too.** You see, if your clients aren't re-booking appointments with you. It has nothing to do with your bodywork skills, education, or personality.

It has to do with what you were never taught in school. The big "M" Marketing.

I've spent years of researching & implementing what I learned to find what works in marketing your massage practice & what doesn't.

I wrote this book for you so that you can have all the rewards & joy of a successful massage career. It doesn't matter if you are just starting or have been in business for a while. This demystified guide gives you the guidance to market yourself effectively in a non-scary way.

What's in this book

- Identifying who you really want to work with.
- Using the Internet to build your client list.
- Establishing yourself as an expert.
- Cultivating client relationships.
- Incorporating Hawaiian wisdom for personal and relational prosperity.

Why I wrote this book

My reasons for authoring this book are both personal and philanthropic. My personal goals are probably very similar to what yours are. I want to have a sustainable and thriving business providing me with an income that can comfortably support my family, and allow me to have the freedom to enjoy life. My community goals are to provide tools, systems, and resources to massage therapist so that they can enjoy their profitable career. By combining these two goals and the knowledge I have learned, the concept of his book was born. I believe that when one has found success, it is much easier to duplicate in others by following their advice than to keep trying and failing individually.

I understand the frustrations and lack of support that is felt by being a solo therapist. I know how hard it is getting started and trying to create a practice out of nothing. I also know how hard it is to keep the momentum going when you have been in business for a while. I do know that you have a dream, like I did nine years ago when I started out on my own as independent massage therapist. I wrote this book to support you during your marketing development and implementation.

My background is hospitality and retail. I started my working life in hotels and have held jobs in every department. I have done everything from scrubbing toilets to being an executive assistant. I studied hospitality management in college before changing my career path to become a massage therapist. I got started in massage therapy as a kind of a dare. While working in hotels, I had lots of friends who worked in the spa. I was constantly stressed and dissatisfied in my job as customer service manager. I was seeing the worst of people on almost a daily basis, and it really started to drag me down. I was losing my faith in humanity and was getting depressed about it. My friend saw my pain and suggested that I should become a therapist. At first balked at that the idea. I remember saying " I don't think I would like touching people."
Slowly I broke down and eventually enrolled in massage school. It was the best thing I ever did! Not only did give me tools for a fantastic new career, but all the practical hours of massage I was receiving during my training eliminated my stress and freed me from migraine headaches.

I know the power of massage and how it can heal and transform lives. I believe in it with my whole heart and have witnessed the benefits it provides from countless clients I have been able to help over the years. I believe that massage therapy and the healing arts are much needed in our society today. I believe that there is enough abundance and perfect clients for every massage therapist out there. My goal in writing this book is to enable you to step into your brilliance in this wonderful profession you have chosen. I want you to have success with your soul's calling the way that I have. I know you may be saying "sure it's easy for you because you wrote a book about this marketing stuff," but I wanted you to know that it wasn't always easy for me.

I have struggled to find my own way, and have tried a lot of misguided tactics. At one point, I was $7000 in debt because I made some poor marketing choices for my practice. I am very familiar with how scary marketing can seem at first. I didn't go to business school, and I am not a marketing major. What I did do is a lot of research, reading, and application. I am a massage therapist just like you who just happened to learn to love marketing. When I started out I was scared too and didn't understand what I was doing. I didn't have any marketing training from my massage school. I did know that it was something I needed to do, so I fell for every ad salesman that happen to call me. Without putting much thought into it and without having a plan I quickly got into deep waters.

I pride myself on being a resilient and resourceful person. I knew I needed to solve this problem quickly. So I hit the library, spent countless hours on the Internet researching, invested in marketing programs and thus the methods in his book were born. I compiled all my own research and applied them to real and practical ways for you to use them in your massage practice.

My hope is that you will use them, adapt them to fit your own style, and share with others in your community. For without the cooperation and action, your business will fail to thrive. My take on marketing is that it is very relational. Do everything you can to build relationships with your clients, your network, and other practitioners within the massage community. Understanding this is vital to my program.

I chose to name my company of "The Aloha Touch System" because of the prevailing spirit of "Aloha" here in the islands. Aloha is more than just a mere word. It is more than the meaning of 'hello' and 'goodbye' which westerners think it means. It is a way of life. It is relationship building at its finest and considering all to be your 'Ohana.' Ohana is Hawaiian for family. It extends beyond your blood relations and embraces all the people who are meaningful to you.

I advise you to start considering your clients your ohana. There's nothing greater than a strong relationship with people to build a foundation for a thriving practice. Marketing is nothing more than a means to deepening your relationship and informing people about who you are. Use it wisely and always with sincere appreciation and compassion.

Mahalo for reading and much Aloha!

"Nothing is particularly hard if you divide it into small jobs." ~ Henry Ford

Failure to plan is planning to fail

When you are in business for yourself, you alone are responsible for your success or failure. I want you to contemplate that statement and really let it sink in for a moment.

What one should realize is that how you approach your business is ultimately what will lead to your success or failure. Being a solo practitioner means you will need to wear a lot of hats. One of which is being the administrator of your practice. This is not as daunting as it seems because it is just an extension of you. Once you know the tools of how to plan for your success, the process of promoting your business and booking clients becomes easy and enjoyable.

You must have clear goals and objectives to be effective. When you approach it from this way, you can start to form a plan of how to get there.

Some important objectives for your practice may be:

- Increasing awareness about your practice.
- Turning callers into clients.
- Promoting services and/or products.
- Increasing repeat bookings.
- Getting more referrals.
- Selling more gift certificates.
- Upselling treatment packages.
- Increasing the amount of each sale.
- Increasing the number of clients.
- Increasing retail sales.

Start by writing down what your personal practice objectives are. Once you have identified them, create a plan of action. It is much easier to be proactive and plan your goals than to just wing it and try to solve problems after they have happened. Because at that point it might be too late.

Always use a S.M.A.R.T. goals system. The S.M.A.R.T. goal is a systematic way to planning and achieving your objectives.

<u>S</u>pecific- your goal should be very specific and clear.
<u>M</u>easurable- track, evaluate, and measure your progress.
<u>A</u>ttainable- goal should be realistic in your current abilities.
<u>R</u>elevant- your goal must be pertinent to the "big picture".
<u>T</u>ime bound- give yourself time deadlines having a beginning and an end.

So let's take a look and how you can apply some S.M.A.R.T. goals to your objectives.

<u>S</u>pecific- You wish to convert more inquiry callers into appointments.

<u>M</u>easurable- you make the log book and start tracking the many calls received and how many resulted in booking an appointment. Evaluate your results weekly and chart progress monthly.

<u>A</u>ttainable- set a realistic goal of increasing 2 out of every 10 callers into appointments.

<u>R</u>elevant- increasing the number of clients and

appointments booked is key to increasing your profitability. The reason you are in business.

T̲ime bound- starting tomorrow you will continuously track your conversions for a period of six months.

This was just one example, but you should apply this to each of your objectives. You do not need to do them all at once, just pick a few that are most relevant to what you want to accomplish immediately and start writing your S.M.A.R.T goals.

Chapter 2: Making your marketing personal

What is Marketing?

"Marketing is sometimes approached as a sort of big-game hunt. The customers are out there in the woods; you have to load up the way with your best ads and promotional materials and seek them out, one by one. If you're a good shot, you get instant satisfaction. The more you bag, the better your business-but it's hard work, and you can never rest. You have to go out every day and find more big-game."

" Building a business through referral networking is more like farming. Unlike hunting, you don't expect instantly returns. Instead, you cultivate relationships by offering others referrals, expert assistance, and other benefits. You form long lasting referral partnerships based on trust. And if you are steadfast and patient, your efforts will pay off and you will reap a bountiful harvest: business opportunities that your networking partners refer to you."
~ Dr. Ivan Misner from the book *Givers Gain*®

I chose to introduce marketing with this quote by Dr. Misner because I feel the first paragraph echoes the misconceptions and perpetuates a fear about marketing. The general populace has come to associate marketing with being boastful and self-promoting with the focus on being gaining at the expense of others.

Choose to market your services in a way that shifts the focus away from yourself. By showing how you can help others, your services then become invaluable. The small change in approach will help your marketing efforts be more palatable and in line with your personal philosophies of serving.

By reading this book, you will learn that the cultivation of relationships is actually the core of all marketing. When you internalize this principle, the easier it will be to market your practice. As you continue your marketing journey, I ask you to leave your misconceptions behind. The tactics in the first paragraph are lies. They do not need to be believed to be successful. Place your trust and focus on the principles of paragraph two, and watch how you come to flourish.

What marketing is, simply sharing what you do

with others. So they know who you are, and can make a choice about whether they choose to work with you. It should never be about coercion; hard sales or broken promises. With that said, marketing is one the most crucial aspect of your business without it your business will fail.

Marketing is not just the physical products like advertising, web sites, and promotions; it is moreover how you relate to your clients. The goal of any marketing is to inspire people to learn more about you, and the benefits they get by working with you. Marketing is an ongoing process and an integral part of running your business.

As a solo therapist, you as an individual, are the critical aspect of your practice. Make sure your Marketing Materials focus on the relationships you have with your clients.

" if you want to figure out a way to grow a never ending, continuously-growing, flourishing business--in any industry--then you need to think like an educated consumer (aka a human being), instead of an eager business person. You need to internalize what every consumer thinks...

'I'd be happy to do business with you... If only I liked you!'"
` Tommy Wyatt & Curtis Lewsey *from the book Appreciation Marketing*

Live your marketing message **Pono** – all that is right, good and in balance. When you do, your clients will see your genuineness.

Are you getting in your own way?

Are you blocking your own path to success?

That question may seem a little absurd. We're not going to block our path to success. But we do. We hold negative beliefs and behaviors that stop us from getting to our ultimate success. The negative beliefs are often unfounded and held in an unconscious belief that has no real justification.

The negative beliefs that I've encountered with other therapists usually take the shape of not asking clients for their help for fear of being too forceful. We feel that if we ask for a sale (asking for appointments) that we're pushing our clients into something they don't want.

Let's take a look at this negative belief. Fear of asking for a sale or referral or an appointment really comes down to a fear of rejection. Rather than ask a client when they want to reschedule, we make a presumptive judgment by assuming that we will be rejected, and we fail to act in order to avoid that pain.

When I work from a place of fear; I need to identify what the cause is. For example, The first time I went to a networking event, other professionals exchanged information and discussed how they can better serve their clients through referrals. I froze. I panicked! I did not introduce myself to the very people who could help grow my practice. At the time I was relatively inexperienced as a therapist. I kept thinking they are not going to take me seriously. I felt the night was a disaster. My confidence hit rock bottom. I had to figure out what went wrong. I don't give up easily. I had to get to the heart of this. I asked myself " Is it true that they don't take me seriously?" My heart resounded with a loud "NO." I discovered that I didn't take myself seriously which I then projected onto others thinking about me. Once I discovered this about myself, I recognized my own insecurity. I worked through it. I was able to make several connections at my next attempt of at networking armed with this understanding.

What limiting beliefs do you have holding you back? Where do you get stuck? What is going on when you fail to take action when you know you should? Dig deep. Get to the true root of your fears.

Our clients need us. They expect us to be there for them. Take ownership of your skills. We are our own practices. We are the product and we have to learn how to sell ourselves. If we don't, we aren't fulfilling our purpose and we won't be serving all those we are meant to serve. Selling is only creating connections and opportunities to serve more.

I developed a 5 step process which helped me overcome my selling phobia and allows me to be very genuine in my intentions, to provide healing for my clients.

- Take ownership of your own value.
- Make a connection with your client desires and dreams. Take the time to ask questions to see what is really important to them.
- Get to know their pain. Discover is what is getting in the way of making them pain free.

- Share your services. When you share your services you invite them to see the possibility of working with you. You offer them a chance to solve their pain.
- Take a stand for your clients. If they raise objections discuss the benefits and advantages they gain.

Here's how I use the five steps system.

Firstly, I have a deep passion for healing and helping people. I have honed my skills as a therapist, deepened my spiritual and energetic connections, and paid close attention to client feedback. I know that I am in the best position to help my clientele.

Second, I get to know my client's needs, desires, motivations and lifestyles. The more I understand about my client, the more I can know their bodies and serve them better. I ask about their job. I ask about their schedule. I ask about their stress levels. I ask about the family. I ask about their life. What do they enjoy? How do they play? How do finances affect their lives? Do they have the lives they desire or is something stopping them?

Third, I ask "What are your expectations in working with me?" And "What specifically in your body do you need me to solve for you?" How long have you lived with this? When did it originate? What have you done previously to solve it? How has that helped or not helped you? Is there anything stopping you from solving this problem now?

Fourth, when I share my services with a client I go beyond what I can provide immediately. I want the client to understand that in order for true transformation to take place it is best for us to work on an ongoing basis. The greatest shift in my business and income was when I went from order taker (booking massage is by the hour) to wellness partner. By doing steps 1-3 I am able to give them a complete healing package that is customized to their specific needs. (see more in chapter 8)

The fifth step is used usually when clients have agreed to working together, and then has regrets and changes their mind. I have found that most often this happens over the price issue. And the real reason price issue comes up is because your client doesn't perceive the value to be high enough or their pain point isn't high enough. It is your job as a professional to help your clients see what life will be like if they choose not to work with you. Always view objections as a chance to learn what you haven't provided your client with to make the decision to work with you.

How to build relationships with your clients

Your relationship marketing success or failure depends on how well you are able to demonstrate that you sincerely care about people first, and that making money is a secondary benefit.

Interact

Befriend your clients on social networks and join in conversations about what they are interested in, and what's going on in their lives. Do not do it with your sales hat on or with the agenda to spam them with offers. Just be a sincere, genuine friend. One person interacting with another.

Be known as an expert in your field and the 'go to' person. Be willing to help others. Free information and advice is easy to share and costs you nothing. Take the time to learn about your clients and what their needs are. Provide them with the answers and solutions to their problems without regard to the financial gain.

By doing this, the sales will surely follow. The law of attraction states that which you give out you will receive tenfold. So be generous!

<u>Be Grateful</u>

Mail greeting cards to your prospects and/or clients to appreciate and acknowledge them. Not many people do this time honored tradition of setting thank you cards anymore. I'm not sure when people got off track from expressing their appreciation. Perhaps with all the busyness in business, people have forgotten how influential a sincere "thank you for your business" card is. Taking a few moments to do this will set your business apart and make you memorable. I found an easy to use online system called SendOutCards. It is an automated way for you to create customized greeting cards. In the two years of using this system, it has been my most powerful follow-up tool for building relationships and staying top of mind with clients.
(See resources for more information.)

A wonderful thing about greeting cards is that people tend to keep them around for long periods of time. Think of the last time you got an E-card for a birthday or an announcement. How long did you keep in your inbox? Probably not too long after you opened it; you deleted it. But think of the last time you got a birthday card or an unexpected card to say thank you for something. Did you throw it away as soon as you read it? Absolutely not! If you are like me, you probably have it stuffed in a box or drawer somewhere. The other thing people tend to do with greeting cards is to show them to other people or display them somewhere. How cool is that! You get the benefit of viral marketing just by being a likeable thoughtful person.

Be A Giver

Periodically send your clients gifts. This can be something to celebrate a momentous occasion such as their birthday, wedding, or child's birth. You can also send gifts saying thanks for the referral or for some other way that they have helped you. People love to be appreciated, and a gift is the ultimate token of your gratitude. What you choose to spend depends on your budget and how close your relationship is.

SendOutCards also offers affordable gifts to be sent automatically from their warehouse to your client on your behalf. No need to go to store, just click and send.

Be Seen

Share video or audio interviews. This increases your credibility as an expert and also serves to deepen your relationship. You see, when people see and hear you, they feel more connected to you. I'm not sure why this is, but think about the last time you looked to purchase a program on the Internet. We all know every info product has a sales page. BUT which is more likely to persuade you to buy? A page where the author was speaking directly to you with an understanding of your pain and offering a solution to your problems, or a heavily worded faceless page filled with sales copy. You may have chosen the latter, but for me until I see and hear the expert speaking directly to my needs and my desired outcome I do not give it much thought and usually click away from the page quickly.

I can see you squirming in your chair and thinking "I don't know how to do a video", but it is fairly painless. There are lots of tutorials out there if you feel you need expert advice. The most crucial part is to get started. An easy way to make a video is to recycle an article that you have put in your newsletter. (See chapter 4) Be sure that it contains material that is relevant, educational, and useful to your clients. You can post your videos to sharing sites such as youtube, put them on your website, and on your facebook. Get yourself visible! When posting online, be sure to include your website address in the information and even embed in the video.

Millions of people are watching and sharing videos every day. You cannot afford to miss the free publicity opportunities.

Ad mistakes you could unwittingly be making

All too often the marketing that massage therapists do engage in is self-promotion.

They restate their business name, their training, and their modalities. You see it in every phone book directory and most online listings. I challenge you to pick up your local phone book and have a look. You will notice in every ad is almost identically the same. No wonder clients have a hard time choosing who they will go to. What is lacking is key to attracting your perfect client.

What you have to remember is that no one cares about you. What they do care about is how YOU can solve their problems. Next time when you are drawing up your ad, scratch the big business name headline and put the solution to your clients biggest problem there instead. Doing this one thing can mean the difference between being lost in obscurity and getting recognition and bookings.

When stating a solution or benefit be sure to speak in precisely clear language. Do not use vague and generically overused terms. For example, reduced pain, decreased stress, tension relief and increased circulation. These terms have absolutely no value to how it benefits your client. Speak to their problems directly. Instead of saying stress reduction say, "neck and shoulders stiffness is eliminated by bringing the muscles into their natural, relaxed state, giving greater movement and reducing the pressure that leads to headaches." You can even be more specific to your target market and solving their needs. "Monitor strain is eased by our gentle scalp and neck massage by revitalizing your overworked body."

Can you see now that by stating something directly to your clients most pressing issue will get your business more attention? When they see how you can relate to their problems, and have the expertise to solve it the decision then becomes easy to call you instead of one of the other generic ads.

I hope that I had impressed upon you, that you need to get specific with your benefits for your target market and ditch the generic massage terms. Remember to speak your clients' language, use words that they are likely to use and understand. Do not get too technical it is unnecessary and not meaningful. Convey a message in a way that they can relate, and they will be sure to take notice.

When seeking to build relationships through your marketing efforts, remember the principles of *Ha'aha'a* and *Ho'ohanohano* - humility and honor. When you put others first cultivating an inclusive attitude about marketing you will gain trust at an earlier stage. This will help you to attract clients who are a good fit for your practice and who will want to refer you to their like-minded friends.

"Do nothing out of selfish ambition or vain conceit. Rather, in humility value others above yourselves, not looking to your own interests but each of you to the interests of the others"
~Philippians 2:3-4

Chapter 3: Identifying, and Finding Your Ideal Clients

"Everything starts with the customer" ~ Louis XIV

Who do you want to work for?

Identifying who you are ideally suited to work for is an area that is often overlooked by therapists. This leads to inconsistencies and ultimately frustration and burnout. We have to learn to be clear on who we are best meant to serve. Our ideal clients are those who have qualities that add value to our businesses and enrich our lives.

If you have been in practice for some time, you probably already know who is NOT your ideal client.
They are the ones whom you dread working with yet; you do it anyways. Why is it that we allow ourselves to settle for work that is NOT mutually satisfying? The answer lies in that we have not explored and expressed who would give us the greatest satisfaction of serving in our business.

So let's take this chance to get extremely creative and actually visualize who the best clients are to give you the satisfaction of having a thriving, prosperous, and fulfilling career.
There is absolute power in your imagining and visualizing. When you can see where you want to go the path that opens up becomes remarkably clear on how to get there.

Sit back, relax, close your eyes (after you have read this passage of course!)

Take three long deep breaths. With each breath allow yourself to relax deeper and deeper.
Start by envisioning where your, perfect work environment is. What does it look like?
Allow yourself to see every detail.
What are the colors?
How is it furnished?
Where is it located?
What does it sound like?
What is the ambient noise?
Is there music?
Is there conversation?
What does it smell like?
What does it feel like to be there?
What emotional reaction do you have to being there?

As you are enjoying being in your perfect work environment; you notice your perfect client is there too. Envision every detail of a perfect client.
How are they dressed?
What is their expression?
What are their mannerisms?
What qualities do they possess to make them your ideal client?

Allow yourself to go back to when you met this person who is your perfect client.
Where did you meet?
What were you doing when you met?
Were you introduced by someone else?

What do you enjoy most about having this person as your client?
What attributes are you most grateful for that they have?

Now being in your perfect work environment, with your perfect client, think the perfect number of clients your practice will need to serve to be profitable and successful.

Now open your eyes and take out and in paper and write down everything you saw. This will become your blueprint for attracting and retaining your perfect clients. I suggest keeping this information someplace permanent as it will be beneficial to look back on it often.

Your vision should have brought you an extremely clear picture on where you are ideally suited to work, who you should be working with, and where to find them. If any of these are still hazy, go back and do the exercise again at a time when you are relaxed and undisturbed.

As your business evolves and grows, you can revisit your original vision or reinvent as needed.

How to find your ideal clients

Now that you have discovered who you want to work for, start to develop a plan on how you will attract them to your practice. By conducting the visualization exercise, you should have a clear picture on the exact client you will be working with. This will also have giving you some key traits that they possess. Let's start by assessing those traits, and how we can apply them to finding your ideal clients

Start by looking over your list. You should have made note of:

- Personal and lifestyle qualities. These are the things that are terribly obvious to the observer. Their outward appearance and how they present themselves. For example, you may have envisioned physically fit person. The predominant personal traits being enthusiasm and drive. This would suggest that your ideal client is into sports or other active roles.

- Where you are likely to meet this person? In doing the visualization exercises, I asked you to imagine where you met your ideal client. I did this specifically because subconsciously you already know who you are best suited to serve. They are most likely located within your circle of influence. Your ideal clients should be people you relate to easily and have something in common with. In the example of the athletic person, you may meet this person through sporting teams, race events, or fitness facilities. If this was your ideal client, you are probably already frequenting these places. If your visualization brought you something altogether out of your realm, perhaps it is time to make a change in yourself, or you may need to repeat the exercise the because your conscious mind was trying to stretch and did not allow you to have an authentic connection.

- Who are you introduced by? This is important because the person who came to mind is probably the key connection to helping build your practice. In the personal services industry referrals are key. Do not overlook that opportunity by failing to ask people for help.

- What you enjoyed most about working with them. These things will ensure that you are enjoying your practice, and it is fulfilling your personal goals. Nothing is more detrimental to your morale than working solely for the purpose of gaining

financially without any personal rewards.
By choosing your clients carefully, you
will avoid frustration and burnout.

Do you realize that the people you already know could be your greatest source of referrals to your practice? Since people like to do business with friends, it is indispensable for you to let them to know precisely what you do, and who you look to do it for.
.
Your friends and acquaintances know you for the person and character you demonstrate to them in person. Your friendship is of primary importance to them. What you do for a living is secondary.

So it is up to you to tell them about how you can help when they (or others they know) need the massage service you provide. Your personal colleagues are valued assets to promote both you and your business.

Your goal is to become the "go to" person when your friends need your services. Who can I turn to solve my problem?" Sure, your friends may know that you are a massage therapist, but do

they know what you really do? Give them comprehensible and precise benefits of what you do and who you best serve.
Tell stories. Give easy-to-understand examples.

Lokahi and *Kakou* are the values of collaboration. When working together it promotes the inclusiveness and wellbeing of all. We all work for the benefit of each other.

Become a **networker to find your ideal clients**

"If you can genuinely care about somebody else, then it's easy to pass them referrals and you can count on them returning the favor."
~ Tommy Wyatt & Curtis Lewsey from Appreciation Marketing

If you are like most independent therapists, you need to put extra effort into getting your name out there and distribute your business card wherever you go. One of the simplest, most effective ways to grow your business is through networking. This may seem scary at first, but building your network is surprisingly easy and painless.

Most people think that networking is only to tell people as much as possible about what they do, and to give out as many cards as they can. They lose a chance at building new and existing contacts by focusing solely on themselves. The most valuable thing to remember about networking is that there is nothing negative or manipulative about it. Networking is building relationships with people who can help you now or in the future. It is not about making sales. Networking is just a way to build relationships. Your networking efforts must be real and authentic for them to work. Your focus should be on gaining trust, and how you can help others.

My friend & mentor Jordan Adler, author of **Beach Money** and also one of the most successful networkers in the world says this:

" There are three factors that will determine how powerful your network will be as it relates to your income and success:

- How many people do you have in your contact manager?
- What is the quality of the relationships you have with the people in your contact

> manager? (Do they like you and do they trust you?)
> - Do those people in your contact manager remember you?"

By instilling these three points in mind when you approach your networking efforts, it will keep your intent in the right place. By having direction and focus with a desired goal, networking will be smoother and more effective.

Make plans to attend a network meeting in your city. Connect face to face at conferences, luncheons and other events for professional development and networking situations will be ideal. Watch your local Chamber of Commerce and local professional organizations for events in your area. Get your business card ready (see chapter 4) and be sure to bring them with you to events.

If you don't have a group in your area or find yourself excluded from your local group because of industry exclusivity. Why not start your own networking opportunity? I did exactly that upon moving to Maui and realizing that all the BNI groups were filled already. I became a chapter leader for the Heart Link Network. Heart Link Network is a national organization that is specifically for women entrepreneurs. I love being a chapter leader and getting to meet other successful women in my area. We build great friendships and of course spread our reach within the community through our network. Ladies I highly encourage you to join a Heart Link Group in your area or start your own if there isn't a chapter already. (See resources)

In networking conversations be sure to ask open-ended questions. This means that you ask the who, what, where, when and how, unlike those that can be answered with a simple yes or no answers. This form of questioning opens up the discussion and shows listeners that you are interested in them.

Be known in your community as an expansive resource for others. When you are known as an important resource, people remember to turn to you for suggestions, ideas, names of other people, etc. keeps yourself memorable to them by being a fountain of information.

Being able to articulate what you do and how others can help you is vital. Too often people in conversations ask, "How can I help you?" No immediate answer comes to mind. Do not get stumped be prepared in advance. Think about all the qualities your ideal clients possess, and ask your network if they
know of anyone who fits the description. Chances are that they probably can find someone that is a perfect fit for your practice.

Follow through quickly and efficiently on referrals you get. This is critical. When people give you referrals, your actions are a reflection on them. Call the prospect promptly and mention the person who referred you to them as recommending that you give them a call to introduce yourself. This pays respect and honor to them, and it also serves as a connection. As you know, people prefer to do business with those who are liked and trusted. Being referred by someone they trust is a bridge to building your relationship with them. Proceed with tact and offer them something of value. A free report, consultation, or introductory offers are good ways to extend an offer for potential clients to learn more about you.

People have short memories. Follow-up after first contact, and then keep in touch with your prospect regularly. If left over a month, your contact may forget that you exist and that you are the best person to solve their pain. You may want to make a personal call to follow up with some people on your list of prospects, but in most cases, adding them to your newsletter or ezine will do the job.
Demonstrate the value of your expertise by sending prospects an idea or suggestion that they can use immediately. You can submit an article you wrote or read. The idea of staying in contact is to be associated with being the person to solve their problems.

Be sure to follow up with the person who gave you the referral with a "thank you" card. This shows courtesy and consideration. The easy way I found to do this in under a minute is to use the campaign feature in the SendOutCards system. (see resources) Do this consistently and your referrals will grow.

Networking is one of the things we do naturally whether we realize it or not. Disciplined networking means that when you meet someone, gather their information. Be sure they get yours too. In order to be an effective networker, it is essential for you to know how you can help them. Find out who they are and what they do. Who are they looking to serve? Make sure that they know the same things about you. Who are your ideal clients? Who are you best equipped to serve? Who might we have in common, that we can be a synergistic ally. Make sure that you are networking effectively by having your personalized business cards. (See Chapter 4)

Be organized when collect business cards so that you remember the person whom you just connected. Jot down notes about them on their card to refresh your memory. Always put their information into your contact manager and be sure to follow up. E-mail is a good, but a thank you card is even better at making an outstanding impression on the person you just met.

Networking is how you can gain referrals, and increase your reach into the community. Although it is not hard to do, you must make the time to do it. Find a group that meets your needs, whether it is a formal group like BNI, a specialized group like Heart Link, or an informal meet-up lunch club, they all work to help broaden your reach and increase your sphere of influence.

"The bottom line is that the Law of Appreciation Marketing has a trickle down to effect. And it always trickles back up to you when you recognize that people within your 'circle of influence' as unique human beings. Tell them and *show* them that you appreciate them. You'll never have to ask for business again."
~ Tommy Wyatt & Curtis Lewsey from Appreciation Marketing

Chapter 4: Differentiating Yourself From Your Competition

"...Always be proud of yourself and understand that it's your individuality that makes you beautiful." ~ Mark Feehily

Express your uniqueness

There is something distinctive and a differentiating factor to all of us. We're all made differently. Like no two snowflakes are the same, our fingerprints are expressly unique to us. Discovering your unique talents as a therapist is no different. Collectively we are all massage therapists or practitioners, but individually we have our own style, methodology, approach, and skill set.
This section is about learning how to find your unique approach and how to bring it into the forefront in your practice.

- Make a list of some of your practice's unique selling points.

- Make a list of your own personal attributes.

Use this list to draw up some differentiating factors that would draw clients to you. Ask yourself, "Why would they choose me over someone else?" Once you have discovered this start to incorporate them into your marketing messages, and above all live them.

I have a personal philosophy that we're all drawn to where we fit. I have always felt that it is necessary to give the freedom of choice. I noticed the importance of this early on in my life when I was a child and did not have freedom of choice. Later it resurfaced again when I had dance teachers tell me that I was not allowed to take lessons from anyone else. I believe the intention of this was to keep the dance pure and un-muddled. What the result ended up being as a remarkably myopic and self absorbed group. I do not think it is healthy for everyone to want to be the same as another, or to follow someone who has to exert total control.

I bring up this example because I've seen how sometimes therapists' can be like that controlling dance teacher. They want to hold on so tightly to their clients and not give them the opportunity to discover who they have a fit with. This is a mistake.

You need to be secure enough in yourself to express your unique capabilities. You should also not be so overly attached to a client that if you discover a client is not a perfect fit for you, that you are not afraid of losing them. You must be willing and able to refer them to someone who can meet their needs. It is a marvelous idea to honor your uniqueness by working with clients that you have the best rapport. This will give you both greater satisfaction and a longer relationship.

In my discovery of Hawaiian values, a few come to mind that mirror the importance of being true to yourself and to the intention with which you work.

***Ho'ohana** is working with intent and purpose. "Do you Hana (just work), or do you *Ho'ohana* (work with intent)?" Let your clients know what they can expect from you. Purposefully and clearly lay the groundwork for the professional relationship needed for you both to be successful. Tell them directly how they will come to earn your trust.

Imi Ola is to seek life. *Imi Ola* is the value that places the ability to achieve your purpose in your own hands, giving you the clear understanding that you have the power to create your own destiny.
(*Reprinted with permission from Managing with Aloha by Rosa Say)

As you come to incorporate more Hawaiian values into your practice, your clients will take notice. They will notice your uniqueness in your approach to how you do business. They will come to feel more valued and in turn will create more value for you by their willingness to refer you to people they know.

Getting recognized

How many of you have created a business name and logo and are hiding behind it? You had the best intentions when you hired your graphic designer to build your brand. While building a brand is respected, it is more applicable to corporate businesses in a competitive market. This is a brilliant marketing idea gone wrong.

What has happened of the spa industry and has become common practice is for individuals to use a business brand. Open any phone book and you will see what I mean. Somewhere we were convinced that we needed to look like a big business is to be credible. We started adopting their marketing methods by building a practice around a name and logo. It is exceedingly common practice to see the business name and logo featured at the top of all advertisements. I know the thinking behind this is that people will recognize and remember the name and logo. The truth is, that without the multimillion dollar advertising budget, your attempts at brand building are useless.

I want you to stop doing it right now!

People do business with people who they know, like, and trust. If you have been hiding behind your graphics, you have been doing your business a disservice. You are in the personal services industry, and you personally are going to be working with your clients. Why hide who you are.

The best thing you can do right now is to go throw out your glossy business cards with the spa pictures on them. They are useless pieces of paper. Imagine this scenario, you go to a networking event where there are several people involved in your industry. You are meeting and talking with new people. You are handing out your business cards. Everyone is doing the same thing. By the end of the event they have collected a pocketful cards. Now how will the people you spoke to remember you and your business? Can you see what I'm trying to get at? If you are doing the same thing as everyone else, there's nothing to separate you from the masses.

In order to get recognized, you must be memorable.

Your name and picture must be prominent on your business cards. Now picture your networking scenario, the only difference is your cards focus on you and how you can be of benefit. How much more likely is it that people will remember having conversations with you? It is also much more likely that because they remember who you are, they will keep your card instead of throwing it away.

Your customers are no different. They want to work with someone whom they can trust. This one little tip of using your image will do more to build relationships with potential clients than any graphic design. When your picture is in all your advertising media, people come to recognize you. Especially when done consistently. People will come to trust you because they feel more comfortable just by seeing a picture. It makes them feel they already you know you. By having a picture, it makes you more approachable.

Become immediately recognizable in your community, and gain ample free publicity.

Give the recipient of your business cards a reason to hold onto it. This can be some significant offer, or other incentive. For example, you may offer 'first consultation free with this card' or '10% off services valued over $50'. You should know your target audience well enough to grasp what will incentives work best for your practice. Always include the benefit statement so your clients are clear on why they want to come to you.

Get into the habit of following the "1 minute rule." The 1 minute rule essentially says, if you talk to a person for longer than 1 minute they should already have one of your business cards in their hand.

You need to find a way to talk about what you do, and be able to offer one of your business cards to the person you are talking to within the first minute of conversation. This can be likened to a conversation you may have with someone at the bus stop or on the elevator. The conversation will end in a exceedingly short time, and you only have a very short time to get your message across. In this case, get your business card to the recipient.

The 1 minute rule is practicing getting your business card out there as much as you can. Do not go through all the trouble of ordering business cards just to let them sit in a corner of your office. To use business cards effectively, you must be giving them out at every opportunity that you have.

Do not be afraid to leave your cards behind!

Every place that you frequently visit, ask if they would not mind you leaving a stack of your business cards for their customers. You should try this at your doctor's office, your dentist, accountant, lawyer, beauty salon or hairdresser.

Try cross promoting businesses that are complimentary to your specialty. Arrange to have a stack of their business cards displayed at your business when they offer your business cards at theirs. This can be a highly effective way to use your business cards and can have positive returns.

Make your practice stand out by being an expert

I am a believer in staying in touch with clients regularly. One of the ways that I advocate is sending monthly email newsletter or ezine. I used to send out printed newsletters through the mail. In my practice, I did this for a period of about a year. My response rate was OK. It was however, very time consuming, costly to print these newsletters, and send them through postal mail each month. What I found is that once I moved the newsletter to the online version my a response rate went up tremendously. The reason I suspect the greater response rate to my ezine; is people will fit time to read their emails more easily into their day than they do an extraneous piece of mail.

It's up to you how often you choose to publish your newsletter. I recommend no less than once a month, but if you wish to do it more often you can. Some therapists struggle with creating newsletter material once a month because it is a little extra work. I advise working on your newsletter marketing materials the same way that you would book your time with clients.

Schedule a certain time on a certain date.

Create your material, or if you're not inspired to write your own content research pre-written articles on a topic which you wish to address.

Don't feel that because you're not a writer that you can't share information with your clients.

They're looking to you as a professional for advice.

How to have your own eZine Publication

Beginning your own eZine is easier than you think. All you honestly need to get started publishing your own paperless newsletter are some content, an autoresponder (automatic email broadcast), and a website for which your potential clients can learn more about you. (see chapter 5.)

Content

I suggest stockpiling some content in advance and slowly give them to your subscribers. For example, you can compile a list of 100 tips in one day and later create articles featuring 10 tips a month. This gives you 10 months' worth of content for one day's research.

However, regardless of any topic you are publishing on, types of contents can be divided into four categories, namely factual content, short tips, mini stories and case studies.

Other than writing your own content, you can get your own unique content by interviewing experts or your own clients. Client testimonials are extremely powerful at conveying how adept you are at helping clients. Third party endorsements are always view more favorably than self-promotion.

Auto responder

You need an autoresponder to send your emails and eZine issues to your subscribers and store your data base of people subscribed to your newsletter.

Internet Marketing and autoresponders go hand-in-hand. In today's online marketing you simply cannot succeed at Internet marketing without the use of autoresponders.

Personalized email from autoresponders is a terrific way to boost your business. When you send a personalized email to one of your clients, the autoresponder addresses them by name, letting them know you are thinking of them. Doing this yourself using traditional email would take you a several hours if you have a long list of clients.

Autoresponders make sending personalized email easy. All you need to do is set up your email template, then select where you like the name to go. Upload your customer list to the autoresponder. Once you have everything ready, you send out the emails with one simple click. You will not have to set it up again when you want to send out another ezine or email.

Autoresponders keep you in contact with your past customers, and to develop new relationships with potential customers. An autoresponder delivers articles & newsletters to your opt-in customer list. It can also be used to send appointment reminders, or cancellation updates. There are many creative ways you can use your autoresponder to book more appointments and to build customer relations.

Automatically fill your wasted appointment times

One therapist that I know of that came up with a surefire way that fills her appointment book every week. What she did in addition to sending out her weekly newsletter; she included her available appointments for the week to her e-mail client list. She does this by having a look and her schedule for the forthcoming week and selects the appointments she wants to fill (usually the least desired appointment times) and then puts those times into her e-mail newsletter and emails her client list. This gives clients an opportunity to see where they can fit into her schedule and what works with theirs.

An added benefit it reminds those that may not be quite thinking of booking an appointment that you are still there for them.

You can send your upcoming available appointments in your newsletters, or send in standalone weekly email updates to clients. I suggest that you use both tactics. Because only sending a monthly appointment reminder will not book you as frequently as weekly updates. This plan is contingent on how much e-mail your clients wish to receive from you. You may find that weekly communications is too frequent for some of your clients. The benefit of using an autoresponder; you can put client e-mail addresses into separate categories which sets them up to receive the monthly newsletter or the weekly schedule updates or both.

The second Point I wanted to make about sending your clients schedules are that after they see it week after week even though they might not be booking an appointment with you on that current week, they will come to you seek it out. I want to change your mindset that you're pestering your clients by sending them emails.

What you are doing is giving them an opportunity to know when you are available to serve them. They will appreciate this because maybe they are not thinking of booking with you this week, but in the future will be anticipating your e-mail so that they can easily slot right into your time schedule without any extra effort. It takes the burden off them remembering to call you or by having to look for your number. The easier we can make it for people to contact us the more willing they are to do that. You also have the option using the open appointment approach by adding an incentive discount or extended or additional service. Offer an incentive to people for the first couple of emails. An example of this would be first of five appointments book received 10% off.

When you do collect your clients e-mail, be sure to let them know that you like to stay in contact with them. Your clients will appreciate your emails instead of seeing them as spam.

The benefit to using auto responders is you get to see the open rates on your emails. This gives tracking of your emails and if they are being read. These reports will help you to see how your clients are responding to your messages.

Chapter 5: Websites and Blogs

"Advertising doesn't create product advantage. It can only convey it."
~ William Bernbach

Vital elements for your website

In these days having a web site is essential for your business growth. When you do not have a website your customers cannot find you and cannot hire you. A website builds legitimacy to your business.

If you are not already marketing your business online, it is time to start. Although there are a few exceptions, just about every business can benefit from online marketing. There are just so many advantages to this type of marketing. First of all, it is extremely affordable to market your business online. Other advantages to marketing your practice online include the ability to reach a large target audience, the ability to reach potential customers all over the world and the ability to customize the marketing message.

If you have been afraid to get your presence on the web, or have a site that is not performing to your expectations let's get clear about what works. The mistakes I see in most therapists' web sites is that they all look more or less the same. While this may have worked in the past, it is just not as effective as it could be. We need to go beyond the pretty massage pictures and give clients a compelling reason why they should work with us.

The goal you should have for your website is to:

- Build a list of people interested in hiring you. A lot of successful websites depend on returning visitors to account for a major part of their traffic. Returning visitors are easier to convert into paying customers because the more often they return to a site, the more trust they have in that site. This is a little different from what the traditional thinking about what service websites are. The previous thinking was that the site's only job was to get appointments, but what you must realize is there is only a small time frame that people are viewing your site. They may not be ready to book at that time. If you do nothing to gather their

information, you have lost a potential client for life. Getting people to opt in to the message that your business has to give is vital to your marketing efforts. Being able to stay in contact with your clients and prospective clients will keep you ahead of your competition.
- <u>Explain your services.</u> Another reason your site may not be performing as well as it could be; it is missing the specific and clear benefits of what working with you will give them.
- <u>Inspire them to hire you.</u> If your website is uninspiring and does not address their needs, they will not act on working with you.

How you should build your website to establish these goals.

Converting Every Visitor into Subscriber!

If a person visits your website and leaves, chances are that he or she will not come back, especially if there are no compelling reasons to do so. After all, we all behave rather impulsively on the Internet, so much so that we can easily forget where we were 10 web pages ago.

The main point here is that your visitor may not return to your website again. If 1,000 visitors visit your website, leave and never come back again, you can imagine the amount of potential revenue lost, simply because they do not return. You should be aiming to convert visitors into your customers.
Before your visitor leaves your website, you want to convert him or her into your subscriber via a simple opt-in to your mailing list. You do this by asking for your visitor's name and email address through your opt-in form.

You must use lead captures on your websites. By systematically staying in front of clients, you will be able to book more appointments with them. When following up with your new subscribers, give them a generous amount of information. Show them your value to make their buying decision easier.

People want a specialist. The more you focus on their direct needs, the more they will respond Do not try to be too much to too many people.

Components for building your site.

Since you have already established who your perfect clients are, (see chapter 3) you should keep your website homepage focused specifically on them. This is another break from the current trend of speaking first about you. What you have to remember is, that clients view your site with the "what's in it for me" factor. They do not care about you. Their first introduction to you should be about meeting their needs.

How your site is going to focus our meeting their needs, is for you to focus on the problems that you solve. Do this easily using a problem solving scenarios. You want to describe five or six issues your perfect clients are experiencing. Then ask,"is this true for you?"

Describe in benefits how working with you solves those issues. Educate them on the value of massage. After you've clearly stated why you can best help them, give testimonials from your satisfied clients describing their results.

Now they can see that you understand their pain, know how to solve it, and have credibility. Ask for permission to have them join your list.

The reason you want to get prospects information is so that you don't lose a chance for them to become your client. Getting permission to market to people who want to hear from you is the best way to build your practice. Having a list of fans and clients is vital to your growth. What it does is deepen the relationship, builds a rapport, and keeps you in mind.

Reward the prospect by offering something in exchange for their information. People will rarely be tempted to give you their information without getting something they value in return. Some freebies you can offer are:

- Reports
- Audios
- Videos

The content of these freebies should be valuable and aimed at your ideal client. The length does not matter, just be sure that what you present is relevant. Your giveaway should be a superb introduction to you and your business be sure to highlight your best traits. Your content is everything. The more value you offer, the more you will be trusted as an expert in your field.

Share your stories and testimonials. People believe a 3rd party more than when you talk about yourself. This is building your social proof. It is the fastest way to credibility. Encourage your clients to share their experience with your business. If possible get a video testimonial. This is the most powerful way to influence decision making. Video has the highest google indexing currently. Not having videos on your website will cause you to lose rankings.

Your second page is the "About Me" page. This is the place you get to divulge a little more information about you. You want to tell your story in authentic and compelling way. Give them the reasons why you do what you do and want to make a difference. This is the story about who you are and what for you stand for. Tell why you want to do this work. Be clear on your inspirations and motivations. Your passion about your profession will move people to want to work with you. When you are clear about who you, want to work with it is easy to identify with people. Clients will only choose to work with those whom they know, like, and trust. Start building rapport early and they are more likely to call.

The third page is your services page. This is where you clearly define what you do and why it is valuable to them.

List your services in the order you would like to perform them. If you have a modality or service, you enjoy providing more than another list it first.

If you have a package that you have created for your ideal client (see chapter 8) list it first. The reason you want to do this is statistically people respond to the first listing on the page most frequently. Put your best offering first.

Describe your services by giving details and benefits. Make the language you choose engrossing and compelling. Explain who it is for and how it is done. Give the reasons of why they need it and what makes you different. Include how they will know if that service is right for them.

It is not convincing enough to list the name of the service and a price. People in general have a hard time making decisions. By describing in detail what each service is, who it is for, and how they will benefit you will best match what they are expecting to receive. Educating your clients before booking the appointment will ease the anxiety of choosing.

Paring your client's needs to your services vastly enhances their experience and the chance of them returning. It is never a good to discover after a deep tissue massage that they wanted the Swedish style.
I believe in making things as smooth and automated as possible. Keep your appointment

book filled by using a scheduler that you can embed right into your website. Clients who come to your website should have an easy way to book with you. Eliminate the extra work for them. While some people may prefer to pick up the phone and call you, others may be looking online after hours at your site. Why risk losing a booking because most people do not call for an appointment after hours. Make it easy and convenient for them. Don't forget to follow up sending them a confirmation e-mail and a confirmation call doesn't hurt either.
There are many services that you can use; some are free, some are paid, I recommend that you look into which would best serve your scheduling needs.

Now that you have heard what works, be careful not to make these mistakes that could hurt your websites load time and optimization. When it comes to your website, extra attention should be paid to every minute detail to make sure it performs optimally to serve its purpose. Here, are seven relevant rules of thumb to observe to make sure your website performs well.

1) Do not use splash pages

Splash pages are the first pages you see when you arrive at a website. They normally have an extremely beautiful image with words like "welcome" or "click here to enter". In fact, they are just that -- pretty pictures with no real purpose. Do not let your visitors have a reason to click on the "back" button! Give them the value of your site up front without the splash page.

2) Do not use banner advertisements

Why give your visitors you have worked so hard getting to your site a chance to navigate away? Keep your site focused purely on your business and your message. Do not offer any distractions.

3) Have uncomplicated and clear navigation

You have to provide a clear and straightforward navigation menu so that even a young child will know how to use it. Stay away from complicated Flash based menus or multi-tiered dropdown menus. If your visitors don't know how to navigate, they will leave your site.

4) Have a clear indication of where the user is
When visitors are deeply engrossed in surfing your site, make sure they know which part of the

site they are in at that moment. That way, they will be able to browse relevant information or navigate to any section of the site easily. Do not confuse your visitors because confusion means "abandon ship"!

5) Avoid using audio on your site

If your visitor is going to stay a long time at your site, reading your content, you will want to make sure they're not annoyed by some audio looping on your website. If you insist on adding audio, make sure they have some control over it by using volume or muting controls.

Get Blogging

A blog is a different website that uses "posts" that constantly update information about yourself and your business. A blog is akin to writing a journal entry. It is different from your website because of the freshly updated information. It is not static, like the online version of your Brochure. The whole point of a blog is to keep the content current and up to date.

The reason to have a blog is to keep people returning to your web site to learn something new, get fresh information, and to simply be updated. Blogs are invitations to join a conversation. To create a buzz about topics, and by their exact nature blogs are social. They make up a hugely important part of your social Media Marketing strategy.

Blogs help you build relationships with clients and potential clients. Blogs create brand awareness for your business, and are a natural way to promote offers. A big part of blogging is to capture client's information so you may keep the conversations going and lead to bookings in the future.

The benefit of having a blog is that it increases your google rankings. Meaning you will become visible to search engines. By continually adding posts your blog, the search engines will index each post separately. The more you have, the higher your ranking you will be. I'm not going into depth here about SEO; it is beyond my scope of expertise. Realize that SEO is necessary to being visible on the web. There are many SEO guides out there if you choose to learn more. The basics of search engine optimization is; the more content filled web space you have, the more exposure you get by the search engines.

The thing about blogging is to keep your content appealing to your reader and up to date. The blog should be thought of as conversation starters. You want people to pass along your blog posts or share them on other forums. Keep the tone light, entertaining, and true to your values.

Some blog of topics you might want to consider are:

- Clients questions and answers- this is an excellent way to get conversations going about your business and how you can be of service.
- Get to know you- this is building and deepening the relationship with your readers and potential clients.
- How to's- give a demonstration video, or explain steps on how to do something. This is immensely popular, and your content could easily go viral (people sharing it with other people).
- Give a review- find an article, book, or podcast, on a topic that your would be of interest to your target client. Write a review of it, and offer it as a suggested read or listen.

- Do a survey or poll- people like to participate and want to give their feedback. Ask for a certain need that they want to be solved. Be sure to give your solutions as responses.
- Lists-create a top 10 list of things to do or not to do. People will appreciate these quick informational points.
- Pictures of clients and their testimonials.
- Promotions and seasonal offerings.
- Give helpful articles or information.

This list is not exclusive and it is up to you what voice your practice will have online. There is no real right or wrong way to do blog posts. The only mistake you can make is not posting or post infrequently. It looks like something is wrong to visitors if you have a blog and your most recent post was last year or earlier.

For the first time bloggers, a no cost blogging web site is a fanatastic way to get started in the blogosphere. Blogspot allows users to set up and host a blog without paying any fees at all. This motivates individuals to start blogging, because the site can provide you with all the resources needed to start a blog without risking any investment.

By deciding to go with a no cost blog host, you may find it easier to get listed in search engines than starting your own blog from the beginning. For example, google runs the free blog hosting site blogspot. It crawls its pages often looking for updates, so if you have your site hosted by blogspot you are assured to be listed on google's blog search engine. This quick access to search engines can take some of the work out of advertising your blog, and help you gain a following with the least marketing efforts.

If your blog draws a large audience, you may want to consider moving your site. Many people feel that being hosted on a free blogging web site gives a blog an amateur flavor. While this is acceptable for a new member of the blogosphere, it is not appropriate for a high-profile blog. Having your own domain can help create a professional image, and finding a company that will host your domain is neither difficult nor expensive. However, it does not make sense in most cases to invest in luxuries before you have a sizable readership.

The application software to get your free blog published can be found at
http://www.blogger.com or
http://www.blogspot.com

Wordpress is the business industry standard, but can be a little daunting to the novice. Blogger is a space for personal and social pages, but it can be a decent place for you to get started and learning how to blog. You can always learn advanced Wordpress once you are comfortable with the commitment of blogging. There are guides and courses available to learn when you are ready.

Chapter 6: Social Media

"Aristotle made the statement that humans are social animals. We like to see each other, know what each other is doing and share with each other. That yearning for connection has driven the rise of the internet."
~ Lee Rainie

Why being "Social" helps your business

72% of all companies currently have Facebook business pages & Twitter accounts. Social media is here to stay, and it is changing the way business is done today. It is the social proof which drives buying decisions. Social media has significantly more influence on decision making than any other form of marketing based on Neilson's 2010 study.

Having a social media presence lets people get to know you online. It is all about building the relationship. Mix your business content and personal insights. Do this because people want to relate to people. It is the reason people are on sites like Facebook and Twitter. Using them is a powerful way to get people to know like and trust you. It also gives your clients a way to tell the world about you. Talk about a powerful referral tool for your business!

Why get involved with social media?

- Relationship building- the benefits to social media is that it allows business owners to engage directly with their customers online.
- Brand awareness- social medium builds "Social Proof" customer loyalty and brand awareness to your business.
- Publicity- instantly share news and events
- Promotions- offer exclusive deals for loyal fans and friends. Deepens the relationship and makes clients feel unique.
- Market research- learn about your clients wants, desires, and needs. You can also learn what your competition is up to.

It is an extraordinarily exciting time to get involved and social media marketing. The medium is so new and fresh and is still evolving. Being active on social media can give you an advantage because you are seen by your clients regularly. Being on social media is being "social." It is much different from other forms of marketing, and it is all about sharing.

Social Media is different because it is a whole person approach to marketing. It focuses on the individual and making them feel significant. It is the art of connecting and engaging with people. You achieve this by implementing a culture of caring, and being involved with your clients.

The benefit is that it increases your word of mouth marketing. This is your most influential marketing form of acquiring new and retaining your current clients. Anyone can be a voice for your business within their sphere of influence. Recognize that people are already talking about your business. Get into the conversation and encourage it.

What should you be posting on social media? The answer depends on what your marketing plan is trying to accomplish. A good rule of thumb, keep the readers interest by being informative, educational, and entertaining. Your content should reflect who you are and what your audience wants to read.

Always be engaged and give quality content in a timely way. Act and speak on a topic that is relevant to your clients and their needs. Answer their questions; it is most beneficial to respond to every posting. Let them know you are listening, and it will make them feel respected. Show that you care, that you are providing something of value and you are not just focused on making sales.

Social media is a place to connect. If you follow the 80% content and 20% promotion, your blend will be balanced. People will be more receptive to reading your content. Do not approach your facebook page or Twitter account like a sales forum. The goal is to interact with people and have them become part of your online family.

Find out what will motivate your clients to get engaged with you. Why would they "like" you? Fill a gap where something is missing and others are not providing. How can you help others before helping yourself? Be positive and consistent in your efforts. Adding value is fundamental to your success.

Social media is like a cocktail party. How do you

think you would be perceived, if the second you walked through the guest's door, you preceded you try and sell them something? Do you think people would be likely to engage with you or would they walk away? My guess is the latter. You have to understand why people are on social network sites. The primary reason is to connect with friends and be kept up to date. So unless, you have a decidedly relevant promotion, your sales pitch is perceived as an interruption.

Social sites are not a one size fits all type of media. This is great because it allows you to compose, and deliver your message in a way that is unique to you and your business. Gone are the days of doing the same thing with the same message in the same format as everyone else. With social media, you gain liberation, freedom to express yourself, and a meaningful to connects with your target market. There are no hard and fast rules about how to do it. Just be yourself and get active.

Getting started with social media is fairly undemanding. You sign up for an account; plug in your information and you are ready to go. Each site has it's own help section if you get stuck. I like to look at the help section first so I can familiarize myself with the site prior to starting to post. It is free to sign up for an account.

Now that you have your account setup, what do you do? Start posting naturally. Be careful not to post any old thing. No one cares what kind of sandwich you had for lunch. Consider your postings as prime billboard real estate. The message you send could be shared with potentially millions of people. Keep it relevant.

The three components of your Social Media Marketing should include:

- Being consistent with your image and message.
- Being of service and value.
- Allowing your audience to be active participants.

The rule of thumb for your content should be to follow the 5 S's

Short
Sweet
Swallow-able
Specific
Simple

So we have covered what you should be posting and why, now let's get into the where.

Facebook is the most popular form of social media with 600 million people on facebook and rising. The average person has over 100 connections, and spends more than an hour a day on the site. The fastest growing market on facebook is the 45-55 age group according to inc. magazine.

How to get Facebook "likes".

"Likes" are what it is called when someone joins your facebook page. For someone to see your facebook content, (if it is not displayed publicly) they will need to click the "like" button. It is pretty easy to create a buzz for your facebook page. Some examples are:

Put a Facebook like button on your website and all other forms of communication. Newsletters, Blog, Ezine, Email, Brochure, etc. Have your clients & friends "like" your page and promote it by sharing within their network.

Run a contest. They must like your page to be entered into a contest and give a reason "why" they should win the contest. The entrant can share with their friends increasing your exposure. Be sure to follow-up with the winner and mention it. Post photos or videos about the winner. This is giving credibility and builds excitement for the next contest.

Invite people to share their experience on facebook "How has my massage helped you?" or "What could I have done better?" Share results and testimonials. Invite your clients to share on Facebook how you enhanced their lives. Why they would choose to come to you over other therapists or spas.

Use Facebook targeted advertising. It can be customized and tailored exactly for your demographics. It is also one of the most affordable pay per click advertising online. (At this time of printing.)

"Like" other business in your area including competition and those of your clients. Engage with them and get reciprocal "likes" and conversations.

LinkedIn is also an excellent resource to find your ideal clients. LinkedIn is a social media site focused on people in business. LinkedIn is my favorite site for groups because the discussion tends to be active, and the people involved have the discretionary income to use our services. You can create your own group as a way to educate and ask questions of people who are in your target market. You can also join other groups where your ideal clients are likely to visit. A key thing is being active in the discussions and providing helpful information. You will build relationships with people, and they will naturally become more interested in what you do.

Twitter is a social media platform much like Facebook. The difference being Twitter only allows 140 characters, while Facebook allows 420. Twitter will force you to become concise in your messages. The goal of twitter is to build a brand voice and spread your online presence. It is an excellent broadcaster to promote your articles, blogs, website, and events. You can also connect with people and see what is being said about you.

How to find new clients on Twitter. Use the # to search keywords for your location. This will give you real time results for what is being said and who might be looking for you in your area. Do this daily and invite those people to be followers. Your competitors may also have lists you can follow. Pay attention to your followers, and engage with them. Make sure to follow anyone who you can network with, other complimentary business etc.

Google Plus is a new player to the social media scene. It is part content sharing, part organized conversation. The unique factor to Google Plus is the ability to add people you already have in your contact manager into "circles" which you can design to share specific content with. I see this as being particularly helpful for business owners who want to target a specific group with their message. While facebook is like shouting your message to stadium of people, Google plus is an intimate dinner party setting.

Google Plus also hosts business pages where you can be seen and found on google maps. It is another free way for your business to gain exposure if you have a fixed location. Google Plus supports Google Adwords, which gives you targeted exposure at a small price. Google Plus is just starting to take hold of the social media realm. It is in your best interest to join while it is in its' infancy.

It is so fundamental to make a decision to get started in your social media marketing. Failing to act quickly can leave you behind. Things happen fast on social media, and it is ever evolving. Do not wait till you have got things figured out to get started. Just start with small actions and build upon them when you become proficient. You will probably find that your social media quickly becomes your favorite marketing activity.

By using social media, you have the ability to turn clients into advocates by keeping the relationship alive. As they share more about their interactions with you, your sphere of influence increases. Most people do use recommendations from friends when making a decision about where they will get their massage services.

Posting should be consistent daily or every other day. Share quality content 80% of the time, and 20% sales message. Get to know your target market and what information they would appreciate getting on a regular basis.

Social Media Resources
Twitter: http://twitter.com
Facebook: http://www.facebook.com
LinkedIn: http://www.linkedin.com
Google Plus: http://plus.google.com

Chapter 7: Freebies: How to keep from giving too much away.

"Imagine what a harmonious world it could be if every single person, both young and old, shared a little of what he is good at doing." ~ Quincy Jones

Do free massages actually work?

From what I hear within the massage community, there is a considerable debate about whether offering free massages helps to build to practice or just ruins your credibility. As a therapist, I can understand your reluctance to give your valued services away for free. After all, you are a trained professional who has devoted a lot of time to mastering your craft and expect a monetary return for your efforts.
Hear me out on why I think you SHOULD be offering free sampler sessions to specifically

targeted clients. The problem I see, and why most therapist do not like doing free massages are that they are doing it in the incorrect way. There is an enormous difference between offering free massages to just anybody, and offering a sampling of your service to people who are your ideal clients. Those who have expressed an interest in working with you.

When I think of offering a free massage, what comes to mind is the therapist who sets up at festivals, holistic events, and trade shows with the hope of gaining new clients and building brand awareness. I do not see being at events as a bad thing. They do positively build visibility in your community. What I disagree with is offering free services without qualifying the prospect or without proper follow-up.

Here, is what I have experienced typically happening. You set a space with your massage chairs and table and then wait for anyone and everyone to come by and get your free bodywork. When you are finished with the session, you hand them your card and off they go.

How likely are you to gain a client from this small interaction? Chances are not very likely. They volunteered just to get the free massage and will most likely lose your information before they get to the next exhibit. You could use this model of operating and do amazing body work all day long, but all you have gained for the day is handing out a bunch of cards and exhaustion.

Now let's look at doing events from a more interactive approach. Instead of offering free massages on the spot, give educational pamphlets or booklets on how massage can help solve their problems. Have people complete a survey to be entered into a drawing for a free treatment. Offer sampler massages for a low price on site. Something like 15min massage for $10-15. This price is low enough that those on a budget or looking for a bargain can afford. Promoting in this way will accomplish two things. First you will be collecting potential clients data so that you may follow up and contact them in the future.
 Second you are giving them information on how you are best suited to serve their needs and solve their problems. By charging a small fee for your bodywork, you are able to recoup the expenses for the day while still getting people interested in your services.

A different but effective way to use giving free services is to use them as rewards. Giving free services as an incentive to refer clients, or to book more frequently is far more powerful in customer retention and acquisition then randomly offering free massages to unqualified people.

The way you choose to structure your referral or customer loyalty program is ultimately up to you, and how it will best serve your business. Some ways that I have seen in practice of are:

- Client loyalty punch cards. Offering a discounted or free service for a certain dollar amount or number of treatments purchased. You know the kind buy ten get one free card.

- Bring a friend and receive a discount. This program offers a discount on services for when a current customer brings a new client to you. You reward both parties by offering a small percentage or dollar amount off the treatments they book for that day.
- Give existing clients a gift certificate for a complimentary service for them to give

to a friend. This is a polite way to get your clients to spread the word about your practice and feel good about giving the gift of massage. Complimentary gift certificates should always have an expiration date within a reasonable time frame. The object is to get the new clients to come to your practice quickly and for them not to forget that they got the gift certificate in the first place. If you do not want to give away a free service, you have the option of designating a lower dollar amount for the gift certificate that they can apply to a full price treatment. Also, be sure to reward your client for sharing the gift certificate with friends by giving them a free or discounted service for a predetermined amount of gift certificates' redeemed by their friends.

- Offer a cash incentive. You can offer a cash incentive to your clients for when a new client books an appointment and mentions being referred by your current client. This will take a little bit of counting and record keeping on your part, but can be remarkably successful if you have clients who are motivated by money.

Do not forget to be charitable in giving your free massages. Donating your time to nonprofit organizations and charity events fosters your compassionate image in the community. You can choose to be a physical presence offering your massage services on-site. You can also donate your massage service as gift certificates for auctions and door prizes. Either way you choose, it is excellent publicity and a delightful way to reach out in kindness to the community. You also may have certain tax benefits by donating your services. Be sure to check with your tax adviser.

So by now you may be worried that you be giving all your services away for free and gaining nothing in return. When you go with a strategic plan, and a goal to accomplish you will find that the few free massages you perform will give you a greater return without much effort on your part.

When donating your time by offering massages or discounts, it helps to remember your Hawaiian values of *Aloha and Ho'okipa*.
Aloha is unconditional love, it is the outpouring

and receiving of the spirit. It is an expression of unconditional kindness, hospitality, spirituality, cooperativeness with humanity, unity, and graciousness that touches the souls of others. *Aloha* defines the epitome of sincere, gracious, and intuitively perfect customer service.

*Aloha is an attitude that is positive, inclusive, and healthy. *Aloha* is a feeling of good service, given with genuine sincerity for the pure love of it. Aloha is a feeling you have because you believe in what you do and what your business stands for.

*Ho'okipa is the hospitality of giving. It defines a true art of unselfishly extending to others the best that we have to give. In sharing our *Ho'okipa* with others we gain our own joy and invest in our own well being.

*Applying *Ho'okipa* to your practice. Extend a genuine welcome to all guests. Give them your entire focus. Be responsible for their comfort and care. Give without reservation, exceed expectations, and anticipate needs. Respond to them in advance of being asked. Give complete and unconditional aloha. Take it as a personal hurt if your client felt that you failed to please them.
(*Reprinted with permission from Managing with

Aloha by Rosa Say)

It may not always be easy to give yourself away, but the rewards of doing so will put you right with the laws of reciprocity. Be of a giving spirit and you will be rewarded.

"Only a life in the service of others is worth living." ~ Albert Einstein

Satisfaction guaranteed or your money back!

"Sales statistics on 'why customers leave' show that one out of a hundred will die, three will relocate, five will buy from a friend, nine will be stolen by a competitor, fourteen will leave on price point, and sixty eight out of a hundred will leave because of perceived indifference.
A customer will stay if they think you do care about them! And if they think you are about them... they care about you."
~Tommy Wyatt & Curtis Lewsey "Appreciation Marketing"

Sure it sounds like a gimmicky sales trick, but used in the right way offering a refund can be one of your most powerful client acquisition and retention methods. What you need to understand, is how there is a perceived risk in your client's mind about whether to book with you or choose another therapist. The reason is that there is a certain level of expectation that they have, and with what we do being an intangible product the client is not certain we will meet or exceed those expectations.

Massage is one investment that has no real value except in the minds of your clients. As a therapist, we are trading our time for dollars. For the client, they are trading dollars for a feeling. The client anticipates that they will leave feeling differently than they did before your massage. Put yourself in their shoes, it is a pretty risky proposition. When you can understand your clients fear and remove that risk, you are moving them towards a buying decision.

Do your best to eliminate the worry, the stress, the uneasiness, and uncertainty. You need to be proactive and make the transaction as calm and anxiety free as possible. To do this tell your clients that you value their well being and if they are not 100% satisfied with your services, you take full responsibility, and they will not owe you a thing. Being prepared to take a loss to keep a customer happy may seem like poor business sense at first glance, but think of it this way...if you make him happy today, he'll reward your efforts by returning time and time again. By, taking a loss today, it will pay off in the long run.

You are to do this because you genuinely are committed to your client having the best experience possible with you. Having strong beliefs and confidence in your ability will impress the prospective client. From their point of view, your massage must be phenomenal, or you could not stay in business.

When you offer a guarantee you are easing the buyers burden. The client then has nothing to lose and everything to gain.

A word of warning in your guarantees, it is illegal (not to mention foolish) in most places to make statements that guarantee you can cure diseases or health issues. When stating a guarantee keep the focus on the clients experience. Something along the lines of; " I want you to leave the room with enthusiasm, but if for some reason I have not met your expectations, please let me know and your treatment will be on me no questions asked."
I hear your concerns that everyone will take advantage of you and ask for a refund. I can attest that during eight years of private practice,

and three years at a resort spa, only one person, asked for a refund. When you look at it with this perspective, the $100 refund was nothing compared to the income I gained and the goodwill garnered with my clients.

Now that you have seen and decided a guarantee is a brilliant idea, publicize it! It does not do you any good to have a guarantee that nobody knows about. Mention it to every client who calls for a booking. Print it on your literature. Display it prominently on your website, social media and blog. Talk about it in every correspondence with customers. Do what ever it takes to get the message out there that you care about your clients, and that you are willing to sacrifice a small amount of money for their satisfaction.

If you do find yourself with a dissatisfied client, Be Prepared...
Let's face it...you can please some of the people all the time, but you will never manage to please all of the people all the time. There will be unhappy customers...that's the way life is.
 When a client complains & wants a refund they honestly want is to be heard and understood.
 With a little tact and compassion, most situations are easily diffused. Follow these tips to keep yourself in check and your client happy.

Be Ready with a "Quick Fix"...
Dissatisfaction grows at a fast rate! Have you ever reported a problem and patiently waited...and patiently waited...and patiently waited for someone returning your call? The whole time you are eager and disappointed the issue seems escalate. Do not do this to your valued clients. Let them know that you are getting right on the issue. Even if, it cannot be solved instantly, they will know that it is important and a high concern for you.

Be Expert...
One furious customer plus one furious owner does not add up to a great solution. Forget about the actions of the disgruntled customer, and keep your composure. Often lending an ear and non-reacting with anger will defuse the situation. Which is much more likely to get the best results.

Be Accountable...
Go forward...take the liability for the issue...even if it was not your mistake. "I'm sorry," goes a long way toward restoring the issue. Once you have apologized for the difficulty your client has experienced, you can get down to resolving the issue. It never will pay to find fault or create justifications. Customers see right through it.

Keep your dignity intact with a simple apology.

Be Thoughtful...
Disgruntled customers often worry their problems will be neglected and overreact to get the attention they feel they are entitled. Let them be amazed with the honest concern you give to the issue, and watch their rage dissipate. You will stroll away from a possibly intense situation with a pleasant mindset. They will remember that much longer than the issue that was introduced in the first place.

Be Aware of the Cause of the Problem...
Once the client is pacified, get to the cause of the issue. Possibilities are excellent that others have been disappointed about the same issue, but have not vocalized it...at least not to you. They may very well take time to gripe to their friends or on social media! Take time to fix the cause of the issue to avoid similar problems later in the future.

Do not let problems get you down or cause you to lose confidence in your abilities. It just takes keeping your cool and sympathy in your heart, to convert a potential problem into a long term satisfied client.

Gaining new clients vs. Maintaining present

clients.

Which is more essential to your practice's development and stability? The response may shock you.

Retaining clients is much more essential to your success. Gaining new clients has a high acquisition price while retaining clients requires a exceptionally low price. If you are counting on building your Practice by regularly attracting new clients, you will learn that it is costly and difficult.

In order to thoughly understand, you need to analyze your return of investment (ROI) and life-time client value (LTV). Your ROI is established by looking at your promotion costs and identifying the costs of getting a new client. Your LTV is established by calculating your clients financial commitment over the course of a lifetime of doing business with you.

For example, you run an ad in your local magazine. The cost of 1/4 page display ad is $400. You ran this ad for six months for a total cost of $2400. Your ad featured a $20.00 off coupon for first time clients. You tracked the results of the ads performance and found you got 100 new customers. The acquisition cost of the new customers was $24.00 each. You then also offered a $20.00 off coupon bringing the acquisition costs to $44.00. Let's say your massage is priced at $60.00 an hour, assuming your first time customers booked an hour session you made $16.00 for that hour.

As you can see, if you only focus your marketing efforts on getting new clients your ROI is extremely low.

Now let's look at your LTV. Your average client books a 1 hour massage every two weeks at $60.00 an hour. Using the formula 2 x $60.00= $120 a month x 12= $1440 a year x 10= $14,400 over a client's lifetime retention. When you look at your marketing efforts, do not overlook the power of retaining clients because as you can see the ROI is remarkably high.

The true profitability of your practice relies on your ability keep your clients happy and coming back. This brings me to another hugely critical point. The more your clients come to you and have a positive relationship with you, the more likely they are to refer other people to you. Referrals always give your practice the best ROI, because there are no costs associated with it unless you decide to offer referral incentives.

So if, you have poor client retention it affects your profitability in a multitude of ways.

- You have more cost associated with acquiring new clients.
- Your LTV's are lower.
- You are not generating as many referrals.

We all know that more clients means more money, but it is actually quantifying the client that brings the most money. This is where most efforts should lie. Now I am not saying that you should give up marketing to get new clients. Just that you should look at where your true profitability can be found.

You have now learned how to use your giveaways to your advantage, and to be confident and stand behind your work. Now let's move on to the fun stuff, marketing with flair.

Chapter 8: Creative ways to fill your appointment book

"To attain happiness in another world, we need only to believe something, while to secure it in this world we must do something." ~ Charlotte Gilman

Using text message technologies.

Text messaging is a fabulous resource to add to your marketing mix. But why would you want to do it?
The response is that text messaging is the quickest increasing method for communicating with your customers. In a study taken in 2010, 72% of adults who have a mobile cellphone use an SMS plan. As technological innovation continues to grow, it is approximated that this rate will only get higher.

Let's consider why adults use text messaging. Adults use text messaging to convey short messages and information. Texting has become a key component of communication. As a business owner, we need to be aware of how our clients can be reached effectively.

The benefits of using SMS marketing and sales communications with customers are:

- Customizing the connection.
- Immediate reactions.
- Appropriate to what is currently occurring.

Let's explore how to successfully use text messaging with your practice.

Last minute appointment openings or cancellations are a highly effective way to use text messaging. You want to make sure that there is an immediacy to sending your text message. Be careful not to be too predictable when using this method. You want the text alert to remain as a special service to your clients. This is not the same as sending your weekly e-mail appointment availability.

Confirming your appointments by SMS is another added convenience for your clients. It opens the lines of communication and can help to avoid no shows.

You can create exclusive promotional offerings to your text list. In creating your promotional offers, be judicial with how many and how frequently you offer them. When a client receives a text promotion, make it seem like an immensely valuable and personalized offer. Do not be tempted just a rehash your other promotions. Think of your text promotion as a reward for those who have opted to give you permission to text them.

And some benefits to your business that TextIng creates are :

Referral possibilities are created by providing your current clients an effortless way to discuss your services with their friends by forwarding your text message. People may forget to mention how masterful a therapist you are to their friends, but when you text an offer they may pass it along to another ideal client for you.

When clients are receiving your text messages it reminds them that you are thinking of them. It keeps you and your business in the forefront of their minds. When people remember you and have easy access to you, your client retention rates go up. It builds loyalty, and the client feels like a valued guest.

Courtesies to consider when using SMS:

Be sure to ask your customers how regularly they would like to obtain text messages from you. Always give clients an opt out choice with every text sent. "To be removed text stop" is common terminology for opting out. Pay attention to your opt out rates. They are an indication of how your messages are received. If you get a lot of opt outs, your messages might be too frequent or not relevant.
Always be respectful in your communications. Do not misuse the trust that your clients have

given you with permission to send text messages. When the client gives you their personal cell phone number, there is a high perceived trust. Remember to honor that trust by sending only relevant messages.

Keep your text messages brief and to the point. Make sure that it is action driven. You want the client to take an immediate action. As in, "appointment cancellation call now to book."

"Everything comes to him who hustles while he waits." ~ Thomas A. Edison

Secret marketing tool: your refrigerator!

Yes, you heard me right. There's a powerful secret marketing tool that keeps your practice at the top of mind of your clients.

Ask any marketing firm and they will tell you the key to any marketing campaign's success is its visibility. The more traffic you have the more likely it is that someone will respond. Hence why billboards and television ads compete for the most expensive advertising there is. The more people are likely see it, the higher the cost.

Let's see how we can apply this to where our clients spend their most of most of their time, at home. All people do the same three things at home. Eat, sleep, and be entertained. I do not quite know of any way to market to people in their sleep yet, so we can forget that. So let's get them where the real action is, in the kitchen.

Think about how many times people go to their refrigerator in a day. I would estimate it to being easily 3 to 12 times. What if I were to tell you, that there's an easy and effective trick to getting your clients to call you by using their refrigerators? I know you think I've gone over the edge, but hear me out.

Advertising on the refrigerator by the use of business card magnets does three things seriously effectively. Firstly it puts your name and number in a extremely safe place where clients will always know where it is. Secondly, it is giving your clients a subconscious suggestion every time they reach for the refrigerator door. Lastly, it provides a permanent form of advertising to your clients. Let's break these down.

Not all people are highly effective and organized. We can make an assumption that when your clients want to call you, they may not know where your business card is. Why not eliminate the source of frustration for them by giving them a way to keep your information readily available. They will not have to fish around for your business card that they have probably misplaced.

Studies have shown the more people are exposed to information, the more it is retained and acted upon. The clever trick of having your benefit statement on your magnetic business card, it is reminding your clients of why they need to call you. Unconsciously every time they go to the refrigerator they will be seeing your name and how you can help solve their problem. So when their conscious mind makes a decision to act on solving their problem, their unconscious mind will automatically give the suggestion that you are the one to call.

People very rarely throw away a fridge magnet. I suspect the reason being is that they have so much stuff that they stick to the refrigerator especially if they have children, that getting rid of a refrigerator magnet would not be considered. I've heard of refrigerator magnets being kept for years.

The cost of creating refrigerator magnets is particularly inexpensive. You can get them custom made by your business card printer or you can simply transform your existing business cards into magnets by purchasing adhesive magnets at office supply stores (more economical but not as long lasting.)

Some suggestions on how to use your refrigerator magnets are:

- Give to every new customer
- Mail them to all your existing clients.
- Give as gifts at networking events.
- Staple them to every Gift Certificate you sell
- Cross promote by having them placed on the minibar fridge of local hotels or timeshares. Especially advantageous if you are an out call therapist.
- Send with your publicity kit
- Distribute to other local businesses. Many offices have a refrigerator in their break room.

I have used this tactic with considerable success for my private practice and all my clients thoroughly appreciated the convenience of having the fridge magnet. One client remarked, that if she did not have the fridge magnet to remind her, she probably would not be calling me to make repeat appointments.

Investing a few cents in business card magnets are an exceptionally good return and simplifies life for your clients.

Building a bigger practice through packaging

If you are serious about making the income that you desire and rightly deserve as a massage therapist, you have to start thinking in terms of making bigger actions and helping people in a more profound way. You must learn to focus on the clients highly desired outcome, which for most massage clients is to be pain free permanently.

There's a significant shift in income that can happen for your practice. Move from selling massage by the hour or minute to selling your services through a package. It is necessary for you to realize that the reason clients come to us is to solve their pain. As therapist, we know there is no long term benefit to having an occasional massage. It is just as pertinent to educate the client on why they need more frequent massage as it is to perform the work.

There's a prevalent fear held by massage therapists that when offering wellness packages. The fear of resistance based purely on price. There may be an initial price objection, but only until you educate your client and take a stand for their health. Packaging will save your client's money while giving them the most amount of benefits. Approach your package by speaking in terms of benefits and savings over the course of working with you. The price objection should become irrelevant for most people.

To have a predictable and sustainable income, selling contracts or packages necessary to build your business with recurring income. What you will need to do is assess every client and recommend the treatment series based on their individualized needs.

"Happiness is a by-product of an effort to make someone else happy." ~ Gretta Brooker Palmer

Go on a joint venture

Joint ventures are most often spoke about in Internet Marketing, but they can also be strategically applied to marketing your massage practice. A joint venture is simply the combined efforts of business people to promote each other and give a greater value to the client. It is done online with the combining of digital products into a bundle or package.

We can apply the same principle and take it offline and use reciprocal marketing with other professionals within our network. By now you should have (or be looking for) partnerships with other local businesses that you can be referring to. Your target market and your location will have a strong influence in who you should seek a for joint venture partnership.

For example, I live in Hawaii, and I am working with a day spa. We are creating joint ventures with businesses where tourists are likely to frequent because they are our ideal target market. The partnership's we have formed includes touring companies, activity directors, condos and vacation rentals.

When constructing your joint venture, be sure to offer something of value that your ideal client is already interested in using. The whole point of a bundle or package is for the client to feel they received a truly distinctive deal. Which they would not have gotten if they had to purchase everything separately. An easy way to do this in your massage practice is to offer a free time upgrade, or to give "spa dollars" gift certificates.

Another way to joint venture is to give incentives to other businesses to promote your practice. In our example, in Hawaii, word of mouth recommendations from locals are valued information for tourists. They love to find the inside scoop. We provide incentives to other businesses to give recommendations to come to the spa. We do this by providing discounted or occasional free treatments for our partners who give us business. We in return recommend the businesses who support us.

Joint ventures or reciprocal marketing is particularly effective and low in cost. Remember it is not necessary to give everything away for free, just to create a compelling offer your ideal client will appreciate.

When you have partners working with you, your reach becomes far greater. You should seek out the partners who have the most influence and draw in your ideal client. Some potential partners for you might be:

- Chiropractors
- Doctors
- Dentists
- Fitness centers, gyms, personal trainers
- Yoga Centers
- New age stores
- Bookstores
- Cafes
- Restaurants
- Health Food Stores
- Tanning salons
- Hair and nail salons
- Activity centers
- Daycares

Your list can be anyone who would also attract your ideal client. Get a little creative in the partners you might approach. You can also do a survey to find out where your current clients are coming from and seek to bridge to any gaps with new joint ventures.

Using "hallmark holidays" to your advantage

"The deepest principle in human nature is the craving to be appreciated."
-William James

A brief history of greeting cards

Sending cards to friends, lovers, and family is a tradition that dates back over 200 years. Although the history and the first card dates back in the early 1400's, greeting cards became popular in the mid 1800's, when the cost of color printing dropped, and the cards could be offered for only a penny. Sir Henry Cole credited with the idea of inventing the first mass-produced cards, which turned out to be a Christmas card that was created by his dear friend, John Calcot Horsely. This year, Cole was late sending letters to all his friends and relatives for Christmas. He contacted the Horsely to ask if he could color, and engrave a 1,000 cards for him with a holiday message, which could then be sent to all. Horsely accepted, and so began the tradition of sending greeting cards.

And so the first modern Christmas card was born. It depicted a boy with a red scarf and the greeting "Merry Christmas and a Happy New Year". Sir Henry was happy with the outcome. He sold the rest of the cards on Old Bond Street for a shilling each! With the help of a penny post, introduced in England a few years earlier, the practice could not help but take hold and grow.

In 1860, Americans were importing most of the cards from Germany, but in 1906, a gentleman from Cleveland with the name of Jacob Sapirstein started his own greeting card business. With a $ 50 loan acquired at a local bank, Sapirstein began selling penny postcards greeting cards at the local drug store, and quickly became a success. After his death in

1918, his son and his wife continued the business and grew to a huge success.
Since the concept of greeting cards has grown, there are many occasions to send them, including holidays, birthdays, or just to say hello. The cards became a fixture in American culture, and continued to grow since. In 1900, the Post Office was having to manage extra 11.5 million letters in Christmas week alone. In the 1980s, the greeting card market had a growth of 10% per year. Small publishers were setting up shops specializing in greeting cards, and in addition, started selling wrapping paper and associated gifts. They were built in almost every street and a shopping center. Today, the greeting card industry grosses over $ 7.5 billion per year.

With a staggering statistics of how well received greeting cards are, it only makes sense incorporating them into part of your marketing with your clients. As we have discussed numerous times, people love being appreciated and in your thoughts. The simple act of sending a greeting card at unexpected times will give you the credit of standing out among your peers as being the caring and thoughtful massage therapist.

Many business owners are sending Christmas cards to their clients. It has become somewhat of a standard practice. Why not make your business standout by not only sending Christmas cards but send also sending cards on other unexpected occasions and holidays like Birthdays, Thanksgiving, Halloween, Anniversaries, Valentines, New Years, Easter, St. Patricks Day, or any other event that you want to celebrate with your clients. For an easy, automated way to make your card sending easier, see SendOutCards in the resources section.

When you consider that reported two-thirds of customers switch from one provider to another because of a perceived attitude of indifference, staying as focused on client retention as much as you do on client acquisition will be a determining factor for your practice. Do not be a victim of indifference. Develop your program of relationship marketing with greeting card campaigns.

The purpose of sending your card is to give a heartfelt message from one person to another. Letting them know they are cared about at holiday or special times. Send with your Aloha.

Do not be tempted to add incentives, discounts or even your business card. Give for the sake of giving and in acknowledgment of the relationship you hold with them. Follow your Ho'okipa by giving the best you have to give. In return, you will receive your own happiness.

"Many of life's failures are people who did not realize how close they were to success when they gave up." ~ Thomas A. Edison

The key to any marketing strategy is *Ho'omau* - perseverance. Remembering that it takes time to build relationships and trust, the ultimate goal of all your marketing activity. Anything worth having is worth working for, and persistence is often the defining quality between success and failure. Statistics say that many give up just before they are about to hit their biggest success.

Ho'omau is the value that will cause you to continue, to carry on your efforts. *Ho'omau* will help you to cultivate tenacity, endurance, determination, resolution, and resilience.

Whatever method you choose to adopt into your marketing plan, do so with conviction so you may reach your **Kula i Ka Nu'u** - your personal excellence.

Chapter 9: Conclusion; How to be a successful massage therapist

"Success is not the key to happiness. Happiness is the key to success. If you love what you are doing, you will be successful." ~ Herman Cain

There are three key components that you need to be efficient at to ensure the success of your practice.

- Technique skills and competence
- Managerial skills in efficiency
- Promotion, marketing, and sales

Your proficiency in the massage modality and delivering an exceptional body work experience is the lifeblood of your business. These are your core competencies and presenting them with confidence is vital to how successful you will be. People will be turning to you for your expertise, so stay up to date on your training and continuing education. Life is a journey of learning. Never get too big headed to think that you are beyond learning something new. If you are an experienced therapist, it is easy to get into a routine of doings the same thing day after day. This only leads to boredom and burnout. Change things up every once in awhile and learn new skills and techniques. This will only add to your competencies and lead to greater client satisfaction.

Hone your bodywork therapy by exchanging massages is with other therapists. Be open to their comments and suggestions. I suggest you do this frequently because it will help you to identify your strengths and weaknesses. Since you are always giving massage, it is hard to tell what the client is experiencing. Getting frequent feedback and corrections will help you meet your clients' needs.

Always work with intention. It is easy to let your

mind wander especially during long sessions. That is the nature of our brains to be in constant chatter. Sometimes you may be thinking of everything but the massage you are performing. I'm not saying that you need to stop thinking, but to just be aware when your mind does take you in another direction so you can regain your focus. By tuning into your clients needs and expectations and by working with intention of meeting and exceeding, you will have consistently satisfied customers.

Managing your massage practice is the administrative busy work that goes on behind the scenes to keep your business running. These are the day to day activities that include everything from cleaning your studio to bookkeeping. These tasks can be time consuming and probably not the best use of your time. Examine all the tasks you need to complete in a day. It is astonishing to see how many things you do in a day when you start to look at them in list form. See if there is any that you could get help doing so you could devote more time to building your practice. You are probably thinking that you are not large enough to ask for help. This is a trap that catches most solo practitioners. Are you trying to do everything yourself and are you in-effective at it? Getting help does not necessarily mean putting people on payroll. You have a valued skill that people would be willing to trade. Ask around in your network of friends and clients who might be willing to take on some of your minor tasks in exchange for a treatment or two. I've traded everything from personal care to car repair with mutually satisfying results for both of us.

When deciding on which areas to delegate, start with those that are your least favorite to do or those which take up the most time. If you spend half a day answering emails, consider a virtual assistant who could do that task under your guidance. Are you spending all your time on bookkeeping and reconciliation? Find a software program you like that integrates everything to streamline your business. Are you overwhelmed with doing all your own laundry? Maybe it's time for a delivery laundry service or a drop-off at a cleaner.

It does not matter where you decide to start, just make an acknowledgment that being in business for yourself does not mean that you need to do everything by yourself. Especially if, someone else can do it faster and cheaper than you can. Consider this, if your average rate per hour is $60.00. You spend 2 hours a day doing mundane managerial tasks. You are losing $120 a day or $600 a week (working five days) or $2400 a month. When you consider it this way, financially it makes sense hiring these out for a fraction of the money you are losing with wasted time.

Marketing, promotion, and sales are the ways that you communicate about what you do. Where your techniques are the " body" of your practice, marketing is the "voice". Developing proficiency in your ability to get your message in front of prospective clients, and showing them the benefits of working with you is key to building your successful practice.

Sadly this is where most therapists make mistakes. They have not learned effectively how to market and sell their services. Unfortunately it is vastly overlooked in training courses. It is as vital to your practice to be adept at marketing as you are at being an expert therapist. Most massage therapy courses give over 500 hours of intense and practical training on how to do the massage modalities. I believe that you should spend equal time learning and implementing your marketing strategies.

The truth is that if you fail only in this one area, it will not matter how skilled a massage you deliver, how convenient your location is, or how beautifully decorated your office is, YOU WILL FAIL! Always remember that none of it matters if nobody knows about you. Realize that without effective marketing you are not in the best position to serve more clients, have more income, enjoy the career that you want.

You may have noticed that there is a distinctive lack of advertising mentioned in this book. I have deliberately left out "advertising" in the text because I believe that by using the personal touch marketing I have taught, you will not need to take out costly advertisements that yield little return. You will do far better to use the approaches that have little to no cost other than your time. I did not write this book to be a "How to place better ads." Any advertising agency can do that for you, and will be happy for you to pay a hefty price for it.

My wish for you is that you have the thriving, successful practice you want. I know that you will because you have decided to take action and read this book. As you read through this book, realize it is a practical approach. Meaning that you should be applying the things you are learning. For without implementation, all efforts will fall flat. I want you to go get busy and have some astounding results increasing your clients, sphere of influence, and your professional reputation.

I encourage you to: live with *Aloha,* do your bodywork with *Ho' ohana,* have *Ho' omau* in your marketing, offer true and sincere *Ho'okipa* to your clients, welcome competitors and advocates into your *Ohana* in the spirit of *Lokahi and Kakou,* and most of all recognize and give your *Mahalo* daily.

Resources

<u>Coaching</u>

I am available as your personal marketing coach on an online basis. I work with only a select few therapists. If you are interested in being coached by me, visit my website and submit the application. I will then have a phone interview with you to see if we will enjoy working together. http://www.demystifiedmarketing.com

<u>Programs</u>

Nancy Juetten ~ Bye Bye Boring Bio. Nancy's book & coaching program helps you craft your message in authentic and compelling way to tell your clients exactly who you are and how you can help them.

Therese Skelly ~Authentic Selling Course. Therese's course teaches the time-tested system are overcoming fear of sales and giving you the confidence to sell your services with pride.

Robert Middleton ~ Action Plan Marketing Program. This book and course use the most comprehensive overview on marketing and I have ever seen.

Nancy Marmalejo ~ Viva Visibility. Nancy's energy and enthusiasm is equally matched by her knowledge and giving spirit. She is an expert in bringing exposure to your business.

Eric Brown ~ Bodywork Biz. Eric provides a wealth of marketing tools, courses, and resources for massage therapists.

Tools

Mind Movies ~ The mind movies software program and allows you to easily create stunning vision boards for all your goals, hopes, dreams, and inspirations. Motivate yourself daily by watching your uplifting mind movie and stay focused on your goals.
www.mindmovies.com

Send Out Cards ~ Is a fun and easy to use online service that allows you to create customized greeting cards and postcards of exceptional value and quality. I have used Send Out Cards for a over three years as a cornerstone of building and maintaining relationships. Everyone loves getting cards!
www.sendoutcards.com/89284

Loopels ~ A unique digital media player that you wear. We incorporate all the elements that promote you, your business or cause into our Loopels. This can include our custom designed QR code, photos, logo, text, images , and/or video, and compile them adding transitions and special effects into exciting looping channels. These loops promote and attract clients or customers to you. We are a Spirtually based company here to serve humanity and elevate conscious awareness on earth. Consciousness + Shift = "Conshiftness" (raising conscious awareness to create a global shift) using the cutting edge technologies of today and the evolving technologies of tomorrow.
www.loopels.com

Aweber ~ An autoresponder system that automates your e-mail message sending.

Aweber is easy to learn & use even as a novice. The service is reliable and gives you reports & tracks your opening rates.
www.aweber.com

Wix ~ Wix is a one stop web design, hosting, and domain registration service. Creating your own web site can seem an exhausted task, the Wix makes it easy to have a professional site within minutes.
www.wix.com

<u>Groups</u>

BNI ~ BNI® is the World's Largest Business Networking, Referrals and Word of Mouth Marketing Organization. Their website provides information on BNI international news, as well as a database of BNI's world-wide chapters and listing of directors, information on how to join and much much more!
www.bni.com

Heart Link Network ~ The Heart Link is dedicated to linking women to resources, new ideas, products, services, and the hearts of one another.

Make connections. Increase your social capital while building lasting relationships. Women networking events have never been so effective and FUN! Find a chapter in your area or for information on how to start one.
www.heartlinknetwork.com

Books

I have read many books that have shaped my life and they are far too numerous to name here. But here are some memorable favorites that have inspired me.

Think and Grow Rich ~ Napoleon Hill

Life! By Design ~ Tom Ferry

Attracting Perfect Customers ~ Stacy Hall & Jan Brogniez

Attraction Marketing ~ Tommy Wyatt & Curtis Lewsey

The Go-Giver & Go Givers Sell More ~ Bob Burg

The Secret ~ Rhonda Byrne

Managing with Aloha ~ Rosa Say
I give credit to Rosa Say for her work on the 19 Values of Aloha. I have included them into this book at various places for your consideration and enrichment in deepening your marketing message and how you view your practice..

www.ingramcontent.com/pod-product-compliance
Lightning Source LLC
Chambersburg PA
CBHW061510180526
45171CB00001B/110